Communities

By Lisa Trumbauer

Table of Contents

Consulting Editor: Gail Saunders-Smith, Ph.D.
Consultants: Claudine Jellison and
Patricia Williams, Reading Recovery Teachers
Content Consultant: Andrew Gyory,
Ph.D. American History

This is a city.

This is a suburb.

And this is out in the country.

How are these places alike?
They are communities!

Communities are places
where people live.

This home is in the country.
The country has a lot of open land.
Neighbors live far away
from each other.

This home is
in the suburbs.
The suburbs have
some open land.
Neighbors live
close by.

And this home is
in the city.
The city has very
little open land.
People have
many neighbors
all around them.

Communities have places
where people work.

This man lives
in the country.
He works
on a farm.

This woman
lives in the
suburbs.
She works
at a store in a
shopping mall.

This woman lives in the city.
She works in a tall office building.

Communities have people and places that meet our needs.

Doctors work at hospitals, helping us stay healthy.

Police officers help us follow the rules that keep us safe.

Firefighters
fight fires.
They also
keep us safe.

Postal workers work at post office

They deliver
mail from
communities
all over
the world.

Librarians
work at
libraries.
Librarians
help us find
information.

Communities have schools.
On the outside, schools may look different.

But on the inside, all schools are filled with teachers and students.
Teachers help students learn.

Communities have places where you can buy things.

You can buy clothes.

You can buy food.

You can buy other things you need.

Communities have places
where you go out to eat.

What do you like to eat
when you go out to eat?

Communities have places
to have fun!

Many
communities
have parks.

Many
communities
have movie
theaters.

How do people
have fun in your
community?

All communities have people!

Who are the people
in your community?